极简西方艺术史

Joan Miró

米罗

像孩子一样绘画的大师

[英] 尼古拉斯·罗斯 著
李慕炜 译

華東理工大學出版社
EAST CHINA UNIVERSITY OF SCIENCE AND TECHNOLOGY PRESS
·上海·

图书在版编目（CIP）数据

米罗：像孩子一样绘画的大师：英汉对照 / (英)尼古拉斯·罗斯 (Nicholas Ross) 著；李慕炜译. -- 上海：华东理工大学出版社, 2019.9（2020.7重印）
（极简西方艺术史）
ISBN 978-7-5628-5959-8

Ⅰ. ①米… Ⅱ. ①尼… ②李… Ⅲ. ①英语 - 汉语 - 对照读物②米罗(Miro, Joan 1893-1983) - 生平事迹
Ⅳ. ①H319.4：K

中国版本图书馆CIP数据核字(2019)第169270号

An Aladdin Book
Designed and directed by Aladdin Books Ltd
PO Box 53987
London SW15 2SF
England

本书英语和简体中文对照版由英国阿拉丁图书有限公司授权
华东理工大学出版社在中国大陆地区出版发行
著作权合同登记号："图字：09-2018-366号"

项目统筹 / 颜冰玉
责任编辑 / 王心怡
装帧设计 / 王　翔
出版发行 / 华东理工大学出版社有限公司
地址：上海市梅陇路 130 号，200237
电话：021-64250306
网址：www.ecustpress.cn
邮箱：zongbianban@ecustpress.cn
印　　刷 / 当纳利（上海）信息技术有限公司
开　　本 / 890 × 1240　1/32
印　　张 / 3.125
字　　数 / 50 千字
版　　次 / 2019 年 9 月第 1 版
印　　次 / 2020 年 7 月第 2 次
定　　价 / 36.80 元

CONTENTS
目录

CONTENTS
目录

To create ***Burnt Picture I***, in 1973, Miró first painted the canvas with acrylic paint, then singed it, to create a random, unique effect.

《烧过的图画（一）》，创作于 1973 年。米罗首次用丙烯酸颜料在油画布上作画，然后用火略微灼烧画布，以期获得随机的、独特的效果。

INTRODUCTION
引言

Joan Miró (1893-1983) is widely considered to be one of the most versatile masters of twentieth-century art. He is often described as a Spanish Surrealist, but even a brief glance at the following pages will reveal Miró to be many different artists in one. Miró used painting, sculpture, textiles, pottery, theater, and enormous public monuments to express his ideas, which have had a lasting influence and show him to be a truly international artist. He was enormously proud of his homeland, Catalonia in northeastern Spain, and of his hometown, Barcelona, which was also home to other artists including Pablo Picasso, Salvador Dali, and Antoni Gaudí. Miró was an exciting artist in an exciting time. The variety of his abstract vision is explained in this book, and by using the activity boxes you can explore his ideas for yourself.

胡安·米罗（1893–1983）被公认为20世纪最多才多艺的艺术大师之一。他通常被描述为西班牙超现实主义艺术家，但只要你粗略地翻阅一下本书，就会发现米罗是一个多面手。米罗用油画、雕塑、纺织品、陶器、戏剧布景以及大量的公共雕塑来表达他的理念，这些作品影响深远，足以证明他是一位真正的国际化的艺术家。巴塞罗那位于西班牙东北部的加泰罗尼亚大区，这里诞生了巴勃罗·毕加索、萨尔瓦多·达利、安东尼·高迪等艺术名家，也是米罗引以为豪的故乡。可以说，他是激情澎湃的历史年代所孕育的激情洋溢的艺术家。本书详述了米罗抽象视野的多样化，读者可以通过实践版块自行探究他的艺术理念。

JOAN MIRÓ
胡安·米罗

Below you can see how the book is organized.

本书的组织结构如下图所示。

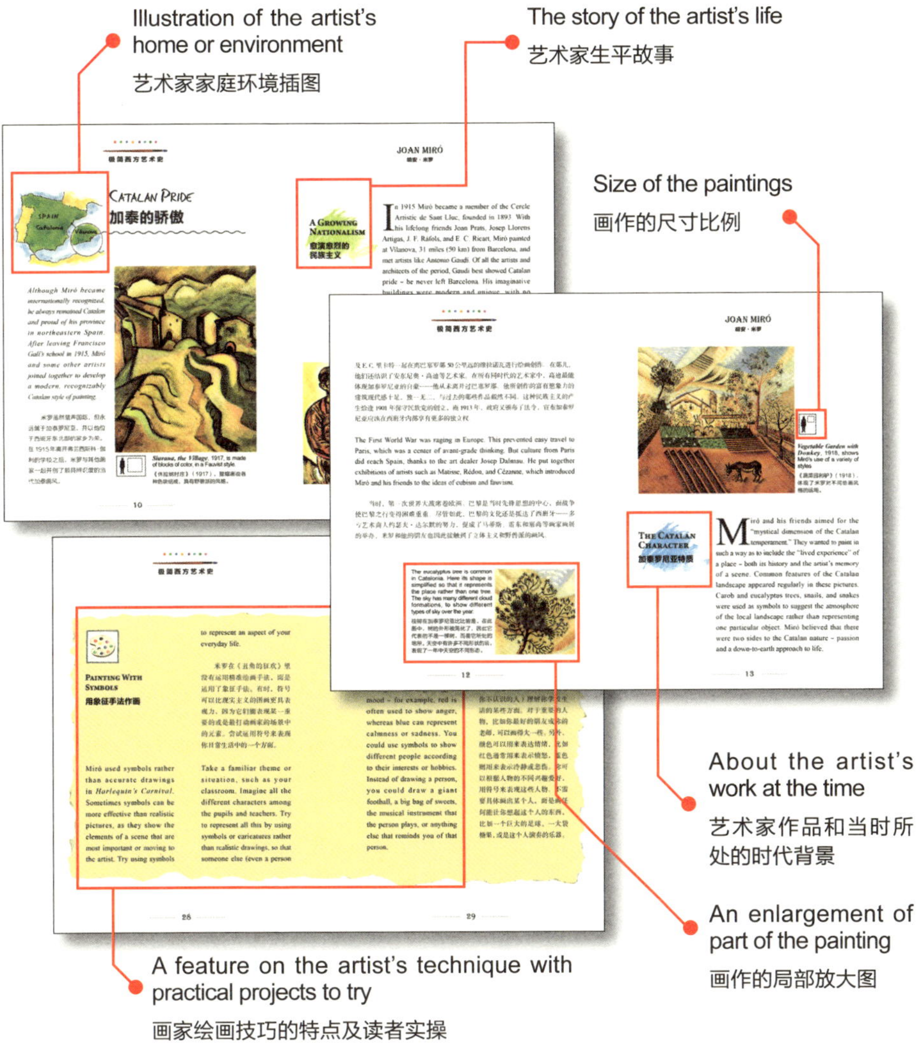

A Difficult Beginning

困难的开端

There were craftspeople on both sides of Miró's family: his mother's father was a cabinetmaker and his own father was a goldsmith. The family lived in the city of Barcelona, which, in the early twentieth century, was thriving with trade. Miró wanted to be an artist from an early age, but his parents had other plans for his future.

米罗的双亲均来自工匠之家：他的外祖父是家具木工，他的父亲则是金匠。他们一家人居住在巴塞罗那，这里的贸易在 20 世纪初十分兴旺。米罗从小就立志成为艺术家，但父母对于他的未来有别的规划。

A Traditional Environment

传统的大环境

As a teenager, Miró attended classes at the Escuela de Bellas Artes, the official academy of fine arts in Barcelona. Accurate drawing won high praise at the Escuela, and abstraction was regarded as an inferior style. The unique nature of Pablo Picasso's great talent had shocked the school twelve years earlier. Within the traditional atmosphere of the academy, Miró's expressive use of color was hardly recognized and, as Miró said himself, he gained a reputation as a "phenomenon of clumsiness."

十几岁的时候，米罗在巴塞罗那的官方艺术学院学习。当时，美术学校推崇的是精确绘图，抽象派画风被认为格调低下。在那之前的12年里，巴勃罗·毕加索的巨大天赋和才能已经震惊了整个学校。在学校里传统的环境下，米罗对色彩极富表现力的运用几乎不被认同。正如米罗自己回忆的那样，他获得了“非凡的笨蛋”这一称谓。

Cemetery, 1907, is an early pencil work by Miró, drawn with great attention to detail.

《墓园》（1907），米罗早期素描作品，注重细节描绘。

The Red Mountain
红山

Miró's drawings must have seemed rough and simple compared to his father's delicate skill. This may have led his parents to find him a job as an accountant's clerk when he was seventeen. The work did not suit the young Miró at all, and he fell dangerously ill a year later. He was sent to recover at his family's farm in the wild Catalan countryside, near the town of Montroig, or "Red Mountain." There he fell in love with the spacious landscape and vivid colors, and felt at home.

This picture shows how free Miró's work became under the influence of Galí. Using only about seven strokes of the brush, Miró has painted the impression of a man hastening after his dog. It is a very different style to the careful drawing at that time.

从图中可以看到，米罗的画风在伽利的影响之下得到了自如的展示。米罗只用了寥寥七笔，就勾勒出一个男人追赶狗的画面。和当时流行的精细画风相比，这显然是一种截然不同的画法。

同父亲精细的技术相比，米罗的绘画风格看上去粗犷简约，所以在他 17 岁的时候，父母给他找了份会计师事务所职员的工作，但这份工作完全不适合年轻的米罗。一年之后，他得了一场重病，因此被送去他们家位于加泰罗尼亚郊区的农场养病。那里靠近又名“红山”的蒙特罗奇镇，在那儿，他爱上了广阔的乡村风景和鲜活的色彩，感到轻松自在。

The Reform, 1915-1916, was painted near the end of Miró's time with Galí.

《改革》（1915-1916），绘于米罗和伽利相处的晚期。

INFLUENCED BY GALÍ

伽利的影响

On his return from Montroig, Miró was allowed to join an art school run by Francisco Galí, a painter whose powers of imagination suited Miró much better than the academy.

从蒙特罗奇镇回来之后，米罗获准去了弗兰西斯科·伽利创办的艺术学校学习。伽利是一名富有想象力的画家，与之前的传统学院相比，他的风格更适合米罗。

A "Crown Of Eyes" "眼睛的王冠"

Galí, like Miró, greatly appreciated the beauty of the surrounding landscape and encouraged his students to see more than simply what lay in front of them. He would take them on long trips into the Catalan mountains, where he would encourage them to wear "a crown of eyes around their heads." By this he meant that they should be constantly aware of the scenery and events taking place all around them. Galí took a broad view of art, and included poetry and music within his works. The young Miró must have felt his eyes and mind opening wider and wider.

和米罗一样，伽利也很崇尚周边风景的美感，他鼓励自己的学生要看到比眼前更多的东西。他会带他们到加泰的山区长途旅行，在那里鼓励他们戴上“眼睛的王冠”，因为他要求学生们能时刻观察周围的景色和发生的各种事情。伽利从事的艺术范围很广，其作品还包括诗歌和音乐。年轻的米罗那时肯定感受到自己的眼界与思维逐渐开阔。

FEEL AND DRAW
感受与绘画

Galí made his students do this exercise to show the young artists that accurate technical drawing was not the only way to portray what they saw.

伽利让学生们做这个练习的目的在于，让年轻的画家们知道精细的画技不是描绘他们所见事物的唯一方式。

Find an object with an unusual shape, such as a pinecone or a crushed plastic bottle. Put the object into a cardboard box and feel it without looking at it, drawing it as you do so. Try not to draw what you know your object looks like, but what you feel it to be, including its textures and shapes.

找一个不规则形状的物品，比如松果或踩扁的塑料瓶。把这个物品放进一个纸板箱里，不去看它，而去感受它，边感受边把它画出来。不要按照你所了解的这个物体的样子来画它的质地和形状，而要按照你的感觉来画。

CATALAN PRIDE
加泰的骄傲

Although Miró became internationally recognized, he always remained Catalan and proud of his province in northeastern Spain. After leaving Francisco Galí's school in 1915, Miró and some other artists joined together to develop a modern, recognizably Catalan style of painting.

米罗虽然蜚声国际，但永远属于加泰罗尼亚，并以他位于西班牙东北部的家乡为荣。在1915年离开弗兰西斯科·伽利的学校之后，米罗与其他画家一起开创了颇具辨识度的当代加泰画风。

Siurana, the Village, 1917, is made of blocks of color, in a Fauvist style.

《休拉纳村庄》（1917），整幅画由各种色块组成，具有野兽派的风格。

A GROWING NATIONALISM
愈演愈烈的民族主义

In 1915 Miró became a member of the Cercle Artistic de Sant Lluc, founded in 1893. With his lifelong friends Joan Prats, Josep Llorens Artigas, J. F. Ràfols, and E. C. Ricart, Miró painted at Vilanova, 31 miles (50 km) from Barcelona, and met artists like Antonio Gaudí. Of all the artists and architects of the period, Gaudí best showed Catalan pride – he never left Barcelona. His imaginative buildings were modern and unique, with no reference to the past. Such nationalism coincided with the founding in 1901 of the Conservative Nationalist Party, and a decree by the government in 1913 that Catalonia should have more independence within Spain.

1915 年，米罗加入了于 1893 年成立的圣卢克艺术协会。米罗和他的终身挚友胡安·普拉提斯、约瑟夫·罗伦斯·阿蒂加斯、J. F. 罗夫斯

Portrait of V. Nubiola, painted in 1917, shows some signs of cubism.
《V. 努比奥拉肖像》（1817），展现出些许立体主义的特质。

及 E. C. 里卡特一起在离巴塞罗那 50 公里远的维拉诺瓦进行绘画创作。在那儿，他们还结识了安东尼奥·高迪等艺术家。在所有同时代的艺术家中，高迪最能体现加泰罗尼亚的自豪——他从未离开过巴塞罗那。他所创作的富有想象力的建筑现代感十足，独一无二，与过去的那些作品截然不同。这种民族主义的产生恰逢 1901 年保守民族党的创立，而 1913 年，政府又颁布了法令，宣布加泰罗尼亚应该在西班牙内部享有更多的独立权。

The First World War was raging in Europe. This prevented easy travel to Paris, which was a center of avant-garde thinking. But culture from Paris did reach Spain, thanks to the art dealer Josep Dalmau. He put together exhibitions of artists such as Matisse, Rédon, and Cézanne, which introduced Miró and his friends to the ideas of cubism and fauvism.

当时，第一次世界大战席卷欧洲。巴黎是当时先锋思想的中心，而战争使巴黎之行变得困难重重。尽管如此，巴黎的文化还是抵达了西班牙——多亏艺术商人约瑟夫·达尔默的努力，促成了马蒂斯、雷东和塞尚等画家画展的举办，米罗和他的朋友也因此接触到了立体主义和野兽派的画风。

The eucalyptus tree is common in Catalonia. Here its shape is simplified so that it represents the place rather than one tree. The sky has many different cloud formations, to show different types of sky over the year.

桉树在加泰罗尼亚比比皆是。在此图中，树的外形被简化了，因此它代表的不是一棵树，而是它所处的场所。天空中有许多不同形状的云，表现了一年中天空的不同形态。

Vegetable Garden with Donkey, 1918, shows Miró's use of a variety of styles.

《蔬菜园和驴》(1918),体现了米罗对不同绘画风格的运用。

THE CATALAN CHARACTER
加泰罗尼亚特质

Miró and his friends aimed for the "mystical dimension of the Catalan temperament." They wanted to paint in such a way as to include the "lived experience" of a place - both its history and the artist's memory of a scene. Common features of the Catalan landscape appeared regularly in these pictures. Carob and eucalyptus trees, snails, and snakes were used as symbols to suggest the atmosphere of the local landscape rather than representing one particular object. Miró believed that there were two sides to the Catalan nature - passion and a down-to-earth approach to life.

米罗和他的朋友们致力于打造“具有加泰特质的神秘维度”。他们试图将对某一场所的鲜活的体验融入绘画中——这种体验既包括这个场所自身的历史，也包括画家对场景的记忆。这些画作中经常出现典型的加泰罗尼亚风光，不过画家们笔下的角豆树和桉树、蜗牛和蛇并非用来表现具体的事物，而是用来唤起当地风景氛围的符号。米罗相信，加泰罗尼亚的性格具有双面性——对生活充满热情，同时又脚踏实地。

In his paintings of this period, the passion was represented by strong, flat colors and the realistic aspect by fine, detailed line. This mingling of styles symbolized the two sides of the Catalan character to Miró, although it seemed strange to many people.

在这个阶段的画作中，米罗用浓烈的单一色调来表现热情，用精细的线条来表现现实的部分。这两种风格的交融象征了米罗心目中加泰罗尼亚的双面特质，尽管它在大多数人看来较为怪异。

Paint In Color Alone
只用色彩来绘画

The Fauvists, whose style greatly influenced Miró, used color to make shapes, rather than “filling in” a drawn outline.

野兽派画家对米罗影响极大，他们用色彩直接画出形状，而不是在勾勒出外部轮廓后再填充色彩。

Paint the buildings around your home or school without using one line to enclose any shape. Build your picture with bold colors. Darker colors are better for the foreground and lighter ones give a sense of depth. Red "jumps out" at you, while blue "sinks" into the depths of the picture. Be bold and imaginative with your choice of colors. For example, we know that a road is made of black tar, but in some sorts of light it may look purple or blue.

画一画你家或学校附近的建筑物，试着不用任何线条来勾勒具体的形状，而是大胆地运用色彩来构图。深色适合用来画前景，淡色用来体现纵深。红色“跳跃”到你眼前，而蓝色则“沉”到画面深处。在色彩选择上，你可以大胆些，富有想象力些。比如，我们都知道路上铺的是黑色的沥青，但是在某些光线下，它可能呈现出紫色或蓝色。

A TASTE OF PARIS
巴黎体验

Early in 1918, the art dealer Dalmau put on Miró's first solo exhibition, in Barcelona. Miró saw this as the end of one period of his life and the beginning of another. Leaving the Cercle Artistic de Sant Lluc, he left Barcelona as he strove to become ever more modern in his approach.

1918 年初，艺术商人达尔默在巴塞罗那举办了米罗的首次个人画展。米罗把这次画展看作他人生中一个阶段的结束和另一个阶段的开始。在退出圣卢克艺术协会之后，他离开了巴塞罗那，力争在画风上表现得更为现代。

A DRAMATIC IMPRESSION
戏剧化的印象画

By 1919 the war in Europe was over, and Miró made his first journey to Paris in March. The many avant-garde ideas in Paris and the enormous range of great artists in the Louvre museum may have overwhelmed Miró, and he returned home without painting a single canvas. He returned to Montroig, and began to search for a new reality in his painting. He painted every detail of his subjects, including aspects that could not be seen but were known to be there. For example, in his picture of Montroig, he included details of the drainage system. Similarly, Miró might have painted a bright sun to represent the climate, but he would not have always painted the shadows it cast, because they would hide objects.

1919 年，欧洲的战事结束。3 月，米罗得以第一次去巴黎旅行。无论是这座城市的先锋理念还是卢浮宫里大师们的名作都令米罗茫然失措，以至于他一幅画也没画就回了家。他回到蒙特罗奇，开始在绘画创作中探寻新的现实。他描绘各种题材的每个细节，包括那些他看不见但知道它们存在着的东西。比如，他在描绘蒙特罗奇的画作中，就加入了排水系统的细节。同样的，米罗可能会画一个明亮的太阳来代表气候，但他并不总在图上画太阳所投下的阴影，因为那样会遮蔽物体。

This style of painting was completely new, and went against many popular ideas of the time, such as impressionism. Whereas other artists tried to focus on just one aspect of their surroundings, Miró

Village and Church of Montroig, 1919, includes many aspects of Miró's subject, including the town sewers.

《蒙特罗奇山村和教堂》（1919），画中包含了蒙特罗奇的许多方面，包括小镇的下水道。

The Farm, 1922, is an inventory of every detail of a small farm.

《农庄》（1922），详细描绘了一个小农庄的每个细节。

tried to include everything that he knew to be real. There was no hint of the styles or techniques of the past in Miró's new work.

这是一种全新的画风，与当时的许多流行理念（如印象主义）相悖。当其他画家只专注于周边的某一个物体时，米罗却试图把他知道的每一个真实细节都放入画中。在米罗的新作品中，我们一点都看不出以往的风格或技巧。

Back To France
重返法国

Toward the end of 1920, Miró moved back to Paris and found some studio space at 45 rue Blomet. He passed the winters in Paris and the summers in his beloved Catalonia. Throughout this time, he lived in a state of near poverty, eating only one proper lunch a week. In 1921 the faithful art dealer Dalmau organized a solo exhibition, at which Miró was unable to sell one picture. Yet he did not lose hope, and continued to paint. In 1922 he painted *The Farm*, which showed his recent ideas and technique very clearly. This was an accurate picture of Miró's family farm. It contained many

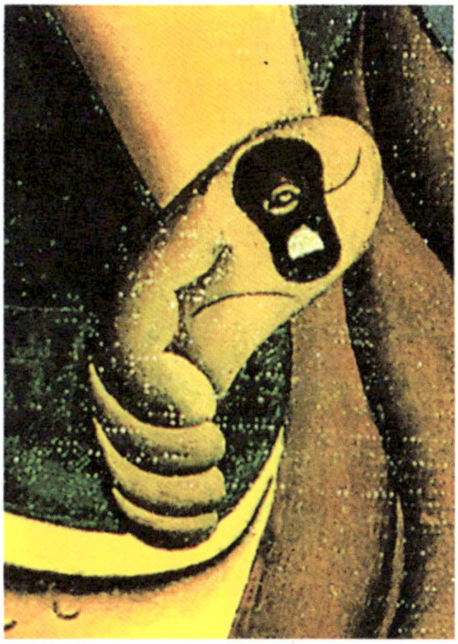

This painting shows the influence of Picasso and cubism on some of Miró's early works. The woman is shown from several angles at once. Some of her features, such as her work-roughened hands and feet, are emphasized.

这幅画展示了毕加索及立体主义对米罗部分早期作品的影响，画家在同一时刻从不同角度描绘了一名妇女。她的某些特征，如因干活而变得粗糙的手和脚，在画中也得到了强调。

The Farmer's Wife was painted in both Spain and Paris in 1922-1923.

《农夫的妻子》，1922 年至 1923 年间画于西班牙和巴黎。

of the elements of his Catalan style, such as the eucalyptus tree. Miró was so fond of the picture, and so determined to finish it, that he took it with him when he traveled. In 1925 *The Farm* was sold to the famous American writer Ernest Hemingway.

1920 年底，米罗回到了巴黎，在布罗美大街45号找了几间画室。他冬天待在巴黎，夏天则待在挚爱的加泰罗尼亚。在此期间，他的生活几近赤贫，每周只吃一顿丰盛的午餐。1921 年，可靠的艺术商人达尔默为他组织了一次个人画展，然而米罗一幅画也没卖出去。尽管如此，他依然没有放弃希望，而是继续作画。1922 年，他创作了《农庄》，清晰地体现了他当时最新的理念和技法。这幅画精准地描绘了米罗的家庭农庄，包含了他的加泰风格中的许多元素，例如桉树。米罗非常喜爱这幅画，并下决心完成它，甚至在旅行途中也带在身边。1925 年，《农庄》卖给了美国著名作家欧内斯特·海明威。

Complete Reality
完全现实主义

Miró used the technique of "complete reality" in many of his paintings during this period. He chose to show the less pleasant aspects of a scene, such as the sewers underneath a picturesque Catalan landscape, as well as the beautiful ones, to give his pictures greater depth.

在此阶段，米罗在许多画作中运用了“完全现实主义”的技巧。他选择同时表现某个场景中令人不太愉悦的部分和美丽的部分，比如同时展现如画的加泰风光和下面暗藏的排水沟，以此让他的作品显得更有深度。

If you draw your room, you probably draw only what you can see around you – the furniture, windows, doors, and carpets, for example. But does that truly represent everything that you know about your room? What about the shoes under the bed, the stuffing in your pillow, or your clothes in the drawer? They are also a part of your room. There are many other parts that you know to be there: the plasterboard behind the paint, the electric wires in the wall, the pipes in the ceiling, or the floorboards under the carpet. All these things make up the reality of your room. Try drawing or painting your room including all these invisible aspects as well as the visible ones. Your finished drawing may not look as realistic as an ordinary drawing, but it will show everything that is really there.

如果让你画自己的房间，你可能只会画你能观察到的东西，比如家具、窗户、门和地毯。但是这些东西能真正代表你所了解的你的房间的方方面面吗？你放在床下的鞋子呢？枕头里的填充物呢？抽屉里的衣服呢？它们也是你房间的一部分。你知道许多东西其实是存在的，比如油画后的石膏板、墙壁里的电线、天花板上的管道，或是地毯下的地板等。所有这些东西都是你房间的现实组成部分。试着不仅仅画出可以看见的部分，同时把这些看不见的也画进去。这样你的画或许看起来跟普通的画不太一样，不是那么逼真，但它却表现了真正存在的每样事物。

SURREALISM
超现实主义

Miró met the poet Tristan Tzara, a celebrity of the Dada movement, in 1920, but it was not until 1923 that his art started to move toward dadaism and surrealism. At this time Miró met many contemporary poets. He began to form a group of artistic friends who were based around his studio at rue Blomet.

1920 年，米罗结识了达达主义运动的知名人物——诗人特里斯唐·查拉。但是直到 1923 年，他的艺术风格才转向达达主义和超现实主义。在此期间，米罗结识了很多当代诗人。以布罗美大街的工作室为据点，他开始组建艺术家朋友的群体。

A NEW VIEWPOINT
新的视角

The Dada movement fought against reason, logic, and traditional methods of artistic expression. It included theater, poetry, political theory, and art, and it emerged from the social and physical destruction caused by the First World War. It had no respect for the ways of thinking of the past. The artists of the Dada movement aimed for imaginative and unique ways of expressing themselves. Their style had no traditional structure or meanings, and so was independent.

达达主义运动是对理性、逻辑和传统艺术表现方式的颠覆。它包含了戏剧、诗歌、政治理论和美术。第一次世界大战造成了很多社会和物质方面的破坏，达达主义由此产生。达达主义者不崇尚回顾过去，他们更致力于用富有想象力的、独一无二的方式来表达自己。他们的风格与传统架构或价值无关，是完全独立的。

A TRUE SURREALIST
真正的超现实主义者

In 1924 the poet André Breton published a *Surrealist Manifesto*, in which he wrote, "I believe in the future resolution of these two states... which are dreams and reality, a sort of absolute reality, or surreality." Surrealism, like the Dada movement, was made up largely of poets and writers who wanted to break away from traditional art forms. Many Surrealists began to write in a way similar to Miró's style of painting. Breton later declared: "Miró is the most surreal of us all."

1924 年，诗人安德烈·布勒东发表了《超现实主义宣言》，他写道："我相信梦境和现实这两种状态在将来会得到很好的分辨，那将是一种绝对的现实，或超现实。”和达达主义运动一样，超现实主义的拥护者绝大多数是想要挣脱传统艺术形式的诗人和作家。许多超现实主义者开始以类似米罗绘画的风格来进行写作。布勒东后来宣布：“米罗是我们中间最超现实的那位。”

Growing Recognition
广受认可

In 1925 an exhibition called *La Révolution Surréaliste* (The Surrealist Revolution) was staged at the Galerie Pierre in Paris, at which the work of both poets and painters was shown. *Harlequin's Carnival* (see page 26) was shown with two other pictures by Miró and, at the age of thirty-two, he was universally acclaimed. A *Galerie Surréaliste* (Surrealist Gallery) was opened in the following year, to show the work of famous Surrealists including Miró, Man Ray, Max Ernst, André Masson, and Marcel Duchamp.

1925 年，巴黎的皮埃尔画廊举办了一场名为“超现实主义革命”的画展，展品既来自诗人也来自画家。米罗的作品《丑角的狂欢》（见第 26 页）和另两幅作品一起展出。当年他 32 岁，已经颇有名气。第二年，超现实主义画廊开业，展出了包括米罗、曼·雷、马克斯·恩斯特、安德烈·马松和马塞尔·杜尚在内的著名超现实主义者的作品。

Composition, 1927, shows the influence of surrealism on Miró, in his linking of random images.

《构图》（1927），表现了超现实主义对米罗的影响，他在此画中随意地把几幅图片连接起来进行构图。

Harlequin's Carnival, painted in 1924-1925, was the first picture by Miró to receive popular acclaim.

《丑角的狂欢》（1924–1925），这是米罗首幅广受赞誉的作品。

HARLEQUIN'S CARNIVAL 《丑角的狂欢》

Harlequin's Carnival was the last, most surreal picture of this period in Miró's career. The Harlequin looks out with a half-red, half-blue face, smoking a pipe, and with the familiar diamond pattern on his chest.

Nearby is a guitarist and two cats play in the foreground.

在米罗的创作生涯中，《丑角的狂欢》是这一阶段的最后一幅画，也是最超现实主义的一幅作品。这个小丑有着一张半红半蓝的脸，叼着一个烟斗，胸前装饰着常见的钻石图案。在他旁边站着一名吉他手，前景则是两只猫在玩耍。

There is no specific meaning to this picture, and no traditional rules of painting are observed. It is a random choice of images in an illogical arrangement. Miró made no attempt to explore the workings of the mind. He simply tried to paint the bizarre yet creative nature of our dreams.

这幅画没有特殊的意义，人们在画中也观察不到传统油画的章法。图案的选择是随意的，排列是毫无逻辑的。米罗不愿意去探究我们的脑子里在想些什么，他只是想画出我们梦境中怪诞但不失创意的那些画面。

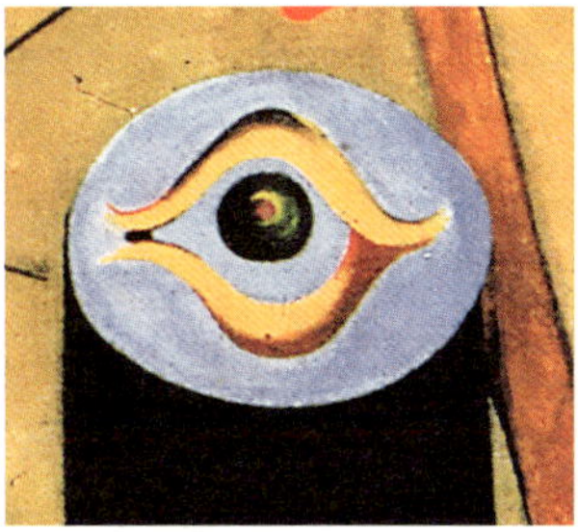

Eyes form an important symbol within Miró's work of this period.They never express any emotion, but are usually included as symbols. The eye here shows that this cylinder represents a person. One shade of blue links many of the images.

眼睛构成了这一阶段米罗作品的重要符号。它们不是用来表达情感的，而是用来作为某种象征的。图中的眼睛表示这个圆筒状物代表一个人。蓝色则把画中的许多形象串联起来。

Painting With Symbols

用象征手法作画

Miró used symbols rather than accurate drawings in *Harlequin's Carnival*. Sometimes symbols can be more effective than realistic pictures, as they show the elements of a scene that are most important or moving to the artist. Try using symbols to represent an aspect of your everyday life.

米罗在《丑角的狂欢》里没有运用精准绘画手法，而是运用了象征手法。有时，符号可以比现实主义的图画更具表现力，因为它们能表现某一重要的或是最打动画家的场景中的元素。尝试运用符号来表现你日常生活中的一个方面。

Take a familiar theme or situation, such as your classroom. Imagine all the different characters among the pupils and teachers. Try to represent all this by using symbols or caricatures rather than realistic drawings, so that someone else (even a person you do not know) could understand some aspects of your school life. Important people, such as your best friends or your teachers, might be larger. Color might suggest mood - for example, red is often used to show anger, whereas blue can represent calmness or sadness. You could use symbols to show different people according to their interests or hobbies. Instead of drawing a person, you could draw a giant football, a big bag of sweets, the musical instrument that the person plays, or anything else that reminds you of that person.

选取一个你熟悉的主题或场所，比如你的教室。想象一下学生们和老师们的不同特征。试着摒弃现实主义的画法，而用象征手法或漫画手法来表现这些人物，让其他人（甚至是你不认识的人）理解你学校生活的某些方面。对于重要的人物，比如你最好的朋友或你的老师，可以画得大一些。另外，颜色可以用来表达情绪，比如红色通常用来表示愤怒，蓝色则用来表示冷静或悲伤。你可以根据人物的不同兴趣爱好，用符号来表现这些人物。不需要具体画出某个人，而是画任何能让你想起这个人的东西，比如一个巨大的足球、一大袋糖果，或是这个人演奏的乐器。

Inspired By Others
他人的启迪

In 1928 Miró visited the Netherlands. He was impressed by the seventeenth-century paintings in the museums, particularly those of Vermeer. He was fascinated by the way in which small, ordinary objects like a jug or a knife were treated with the same attention to detail as the main subject.

1928 年，米罗访问了荷兰。博物馆里 17 世纪的画作，尤其是维米尔的作品，给他留下了深刻的印象。在维米尔的作品中，一个壶或一把刀等又小又平常的东西也得到了细致的刻画，画家对它们的关注一点都不亚于主体事物。

Tensions Within Surrealism
超现实主义内部的矛盾

The Surrealist movement had grown stronger after 1925, but cracks had begun to appear within it. Political arguments, and the risk of offending André Breton, drove Miró away from the group. He was treated with growing suspicion for holding his own views, which he tended to keep to himself.

超现实主义运动在 1925 年以后日益壮大，但内部开始出现裂痕。政治上的争论，再加上可能冒犯安德烈·布勒东的风险，使得米罗被迫远离这个群体。他坚持己见，却引来了越来越多的怀疑。

When Miró and the artist Max Ernst created a stage set for the opera *Romeo and Juliet* in 1926, Breton staged a demonstration outside the theater. He accused Miró and Ernst of indulging in middle-class, meaningless creative activities that completely contradicted the revolutionary spirit of the surrealist movement.

1926 年，米罗和艺术家马克斯·恩斯特为歌剧《罗密欧与朱丽叶》特别打造了一个舞台。布勒东在剧院外发起了示威，谴责米罗和恩斯特沉湎于中产阶级毫无意义的创造活动，他认为这有悖于超现实主义运动的革命精神。

ART ON MANY LEVELS
多种层面的艺术

Miró went to the Netherlands, where his style began to change once again. He aimed to combine the accurate detail used by the Dutch master painters with his own abstract style. This seems to be a contradiction: how can a detail be recognized as a detail once it is abstracted? The letter in the picture on page 32 is not a detailed drawing but an abstract image representing a letter. However, the letter is a detailed part of an existing picture, *Mrs. Mills Reading a Letter*, painted by George Engleheart in 1750. Miró's portrayal of the letter is therefore recognizable as an abstraction of another artist's detail.

米罗去了荷兰，在那里他再一次改变了风格。他意图将荷兰绘画大师的精细画风和他自身的抽象风格结合起来。这看起来似乎是矛盾的：一个细节一旦抽象化，怎么还能叫作细节呢？第 32 页这幅画中的信不是用精细手法描绘的，而是由抽象的图案来表示。然而，这封信是画作《米勒夫人阅读信件》的一个精细部分。这幅画由乔治·恩格哈特绘于 1750 年，米罗对信的描绘则可以看作对恩格哈特作品细节的抽象表达。

A Portrait of Mrs. Mills in 1750, painted in 1929, was based on a painting by Engleheart.

《1750 年的米勒夫人肖像》（1929），取材于恩格哈特的作品。

INFLUENCED BY THE MASTERS
大师的影响

Miró's *Dutch Interior I* was also an abstracted version of an existing painting. Its composition and features were taken directly from a painting by the Dutch master Hendrick Martensz Sorgh (1610-1670), called *The Lute Player*. Miró painted in such a way for a short time, but he quickly moved on to even greater degrees of abstraction.

米罗的《荷兰室内画（一）》同样是对现有作品的抽象化创作。它的构图和特点直接取材于荷兰大画家亨德里克·马丁斯·索格（1610—1670）的作品《琵琶手》。米罗以这种方式进行了一段时间的创作，然后他很快就转向了更为抽象的画风。

Dutch Interior I, 1928, was based on *The Lute Player* by H. M. Sorgh.

《荷兰室内画（一）》（1928），取材于H. M. 索格的作品《琵琶手》。

Miró has summarized the character of the spaniel in Sorgh's painting in a very amusing way. In the original picture, the dog is shown to be pampered and rather stupid. Miró has shown the dog smoking a pipe and staring blankly out at the viewer.

米罗以一种有趣的方式归纳了索格作品中西班牙猎狗的特征。在原画中，狗看上去娇生惯养且愚笨不堪；而在米罗笔下，狗则叼着烟斗，茫然地盯着观众。

MARRIAGE AND FAMILY
婚姻和家庭

For two years Miró had lived on the rue Tourlaque in Paris. In 1929, he married Pilar Juncosa, who gave birth to a daughter, Maria Dolores, in 1931. The family continued to live in Paris, but they had to move to a cheaper area of the city because a call in the demand for modern art had left Miró short of money. Every summer the family went to Catalonia or to Palma on Majorca, where Miró's mother owned some property.

米罗在巴黎图拉克大街居住了两年。1929 年，他和皮拉尔·琼珂萨结婚。1931 年，两人生下一女玛利亚·多罗茜。之后，一家人仍然住在巴黎，但因为对现代艺术的追求导致米罗手头拮据，他们不得不搬到市里比较便宜的区域。每年夏天，一家人都会去加泰罗尼亚或马略卡岛上的帕尔马待一阵，米罗的母亲在帕尔马拥有一些房产。

ABSTRACT A PICTURE
对图画做抽象处理

Find a famous picture by a master painter, such as Botticelli's *The Birth of Venus* or da Vinci's *Mona Lisa.*

找一幅大师的名作，比如波提切利的《维纳斯的诞生》或达·芬奇的《蒙娜丽莎》。

Make your own version by replacing the main features of the picture with symbols or exaggerated details. Decide which elements of the original picture are the most important or interesting to you, and make them prominent in your version with exaggeration or bold colors. For example, you may find the background to the *Mona Lisa* fascinating, so emphasize some of the features within it – there are craggy mountains, wide rivers, and a bridge. Or you could emphasize Venus's flowing red hair, the angels flying beside her or the flowers being carried in the wind.

用符号或夸张的细节来替换名画的主要特征，从而形成你自己的版本。自行决定原画中对你来说最重要或你最感兴趣的地方，在你的版本中用夸张的方式或大胆的色彩来突出这些地方。例如，你可能会觉得《蒙娜丽莎》的背景很吸引人，那么你就可以强调其中的某些特征，如陡峭的山、宽阔的河，以及小桥。或者，你可以强调维纳斯飘逸的红发、在她身边飞舞的天使，或风中飘荡的花瓣等。

A similar technique of redrawing well-known works of art or people is often used in satirical cartoons in newspapers. A cartoonist may abstract certain features of a public figure, for example, by making them enormously large. The cartoon is funny because the viewer recognizes the exaggerated features as a representation of someone well known. Try making your own cartoons of well-known people.

类似重绘知名画作或人物的技巧也广泛应用于报纸上的讽刺卡通画。卡通画家会用诸如放大的手法把公众人物的某些特征抽象化。因为观众能辨认出夸张的部分是某个知名人物的特征，所以卡通画便有了搞笑的效果。试着自己画几幅知名人物的卡通画吧。

WAR IN ART AND LIFE
艺术之战和现实之战

Miró now began to experiment with the traditional medium in which artists had worked for centuries – paint and canvas. This was the beginning of a period in which he "assassinated painting" by using colored paper, cloth, or any found objects ("objets trouvés") to make pictures.

至此，米罗开始革新艺术家们在几个世纪的时间里使用的传统绘画介质——颜料和油画帆布。他用彩色纸、布或任何可以找到的物体（“拾得物”）来作画，并从此开始了“暗杀绘画”的阶段。

THE SPANISH CIVIL WAR
西班牙内战

In 1933 Miró returned to Barcelona with his family, to spend some time working on his paintings, but his stay was cut short. Spanish politics were forced to dangerous extremes in the 1930s, with the growth of the opposing Fascist and Communist movements. In July 1936, a grueling civil war broke out in Spain, between the Fascists under General Franco and the Communist-led Republicans. Miró was a Republican, like many people in Catalonia, and the war forced him and his family to leave Barcelona for Paris again.

1933年，米罗和家人一起回到巴塞罗那，想花点时间作画，但他不得不缩短在那里停留的时间。20世纪30年代，由于法西斯反对势力的日益壮大以及共产主义运动的茁壮发展，西班牙的政客们被迫铤而走险。1936年7月，激烈的内战在西班牙爆发，交战双方分别为以佛朗哥将军为首的法西斯军队和由共产主义者领导的共和党人。和许多加泰罗尼亚人一样，米罗也是一名共和党人。战争迫使他和家人离开巴塞罗那，再次回到了巴黎。

YEARS OF HARDSHIP
艰难岁月

Economic depression had damaged the art market in Europe, leading to several years of poverty for Miró and his family. This difficult life and the cruel nature of the war in Spain affected Miró greatly. What he described as his "wild paintings" were produced during this period. These pictures featured

Painting Based on a Collage, 1933.
《在拼贴画基础上创作的油画》（1933）

large, monstrous beings formed by harsh lines and ugly colors. In the Paris International Exhibition of 1937, one such painting, a mural called *The Reaper*, was displayed next to Picasso's famous criticism of war, *Guernica*. It covered a whole wall of the large Spanish Pavilion.

经济萧条破坏了欧洲的艺术市场，米罗和家人也因此度过了好几年贫困的时光。生活的艰难和西班牙内战的残酷极大地影响了米罗，被他称为“野性绘画”的风格正是在这一时期形成的。这些画的特点是都有巨大的、畸形的物体，由粗糙的线条和丑陋的色彩构成。1937 年的巴黎国际画展展出了体现这一风格的壁画——《收割者》，它和毕加索那幅抨击战争的名画《格尔尼卡》陈列在一起。这幅画占据了庞大的西班牙展馆的整面墙壁。

THE END OF THE DREAM
梦想的终结

The main image of *The Reaper* is a peasant from Catalonia, a subject that had been featured in many of Miró's previous paintings. However, this picture did not represent a harmonious or pleasant view of Catalonia, but demonstrated Miró's anger at the war. Miró showed the peasant shouting violently, as if voicing his rage about the war and his determination not to be downtrodden. Despite the picture's vast size, however, it mysteriously disappeared during the journey back from the exhibition.

《收割者》的主要人物是一名加泰罗尼亚农民，这一主题经常出现在米罗之前的画作中。然而，这幅画并未呈现加泰罗尼亚和谐或令人愉悦的景致，而是

Throughout Miró's paintings, his lines were usually curvy and gentle. In the Civil War period there appeared a new sense of horror, which caused him to paint shocking images such as this screaming woman.

纵观米罗的画作，他所使用的线条通常都是曲线，用笔比较柔和。在西班牙内战期间出现了一种新的恐惧感，这种感觉促使他画出了令人触目惊心的形象，比如这个尖叫的女人。

表现了米罗对战争的愤怒。在米罗笔下，这个农民充满激情地叫喊着，像要咆哮出他对战争的狂怒以及不被践踏的决心。尽管这幅画面积巨大，却在画展结束后被运回的途中神秘地失踪了。

"AIDEZ L'ESPAGNE"
"帮助西班牙"

Miró became further involved with contemporary events when he designed a powerful poster entitled *Aidez l'Espagne* ("Help Spain"). The poster was sold across Europe for one

Flame in Space and Female Nude, 1932, is one of Miró's "wild paintings."

《空间中的火花和女性裸体》（1932），米罗"野性绘画"的代表作之一。

French franc per copy, to raise money for the Spanish Republican movement. Miró said at the time: "In the present struggle I can see, on the one hand, the Fascists as an antagonistic force, on the other, the people." This sympathy with the Spanish people is clear in all his major works painted during the Spanish Civil War.

米罗设计了一幅名为《帮助西班牙》的富有震撼力的海报，以此更深入地参与那个时期的社会政治活动。这幅海报的复制品在全欧洲以一法郎一张的价格出售，从而为西班牙共和党运动募集资金。米罗在那时说："在目前的抗争中，我能看到一方是作为敌对力量的法西斯主义者，而另一方是人民。"米罗在西班牙内战期间所创作的主要作品都清晰地体现了他对西班牙人民的同情。

REPRESENTING THE PEOPLE
代表人民

In his works of this period, Miró captured the moods of all the people of Spain. His paintings were reflections of the hopes, fears, and dreams of everybody in the country; they were not intended to deliver his personal intellectual or political message.

在这一阶段的作品中，米罗抓住了西班牙各类人群的各种情绪。他的画作表现了西班牙国内每一个人的希望、恐惧和梦想，而不是用来表现米罗本人的才智或政治立场的。

Flat Colors
单调平面色

Make a simple design of a portrait or a street scene, then paint the picture using flat areas of plain color.

简单设计一幅肖像画或街景画，然后用素色填充的平面区域来作画。

Choose strong colors such as Chinese red, cobalt blue, or chrome yellow, and lay them down as areas of pure color. Remember that different colors and types of paint have different textures and impact. Allow the paper, canvas, or board underneath your color to show through in places.

选择一些浓烈的颜色，比如中国红、钴蓝色或铬黄色，然后用这些纯色填充相关区域。记住，不同的颜色和颜料类型有着不同的质地和效果。让纸、画布或画板在适当的地方裸露出来，不要上色。

CONSTELLATIONS
《星座》

In 1939 the rise of the German Nazi Party threatened another major war in Europe. Miró moved his family from Paris to Varengeville, Normandy, in the following year. The stormy skies and dramatic beaches of Normandy restored his faith in nature and inspired yet another change in his artistic style.

1939 年，德国纳粹党的崛起导致了欧洲另一场大战的爆发。次年，米罗和家人从巴黎搬到了诺曼底的瓦亨芝维拉。诺曼底的暴风雨和惊险刺激的海滩让米罗重拾对自然的信仰，也激发了他艺术风格上的又一次转变。

Painting with an Art Nouveau Frame, 1943.
《画框为新艺术风格的油画》（1943）

The Flight From The Nazis
躲避纳粹

Miró later said of his time in Normandy: "I felt a deep desire to escape. I deliberately shut up my mind. The night, music, and the stars began to play an increasingly important role in my pictures." At this time he began a series of pictures known as the *Constellations*. However, in the middle of his work he was forced to escape the advancing German army by moving his family to Barcelona.

后来，米罗这样评价他在诺曼底的生活："我深深地渴望逃离。我故意封闭自己的意识。黑夜、音乐和星星开始在我的画作中占据越来越重要的地位。"在这一时期，他开始创作一系列被称为《星座》的组画。然而在创作期间，由于德军入侵，他被迫带着家人逃离诺曼底，又搬回了巴塞罗那。

The family raced to Paris, where they boarded the last train to leave for Barcelona before the Nazis overran the city. Miró could not stay in Barcelona. His *Aidez l'Espagne* poster had displayed his Republican feelings too strongly, and the new Fascist government refused to accept him. He moved his family to Palma, on Majorca.

米罗一家迅速赶往巴黎，坐上了纳粹占领巴黎前最后一班开往巴塞罗那的火车。然而，米罗不能待在巴塞罗那。因为他创作的海报《帮助西班牙》过分强烈地传达了他的共和党人理念，所以新的法西斯政府拒绝接受他。他只能带着家人搬到了马略卡岛上的帕尔马。

A Surprising Harmony
出人意料的和谐

The *Constellations* were finished in Palma, and showed none of the harsh lines of Miró's "wild paintings." The positions of the figures were not aggressive, and the compositions were evenly spread with balanced colors. Miró composed the *Constellations* by first drawing a random line on the paper. He then allowed himself to find shapes and figures within the line, which he filled in and decorated with paint. By the time Miró and his family were able to move back to Barcelona, in 1942, he was using a unique visual language.

《星座》在帕尔马创作完毕。在这一系列的绘画中，人们丝毫看不到米罗“野性绘画”中运用的粗糙线条。人物的姿态不再具有攻击性，整个构图铺满了平衡的色彩。米罗在创作《星座》时，首先在纸上随意地画出线条，然后找出线条构成的形状和图案，再用颜色填充和装饰它们。1942 年，当米罗和家人得以返回巴塞罗那时，他正在采用一种独特的视觉语言。

To create ***Woman Encircled by the Flight of a Bird*** in 1941, Miró drew a random line, then filled it in with color.

《被飞行的鸟包围的女人》（1941），为创作这幅画，米罗先随意地画了一条线，然后为其填充了颜色。

Back To A Harsher Vision
回归更粗犷的视觉效果

Miró soon returned to a stronger style, however. The *Barcelona Suite* contained fifty harsh lithographs which revealed his feelings of anguish about the Second World War.

然而，米罗很快就回归了一种更强烈的风格。《巴塞罗那组图》包含了 50 幅粗犷的石版画，这些画展现了第二次世界大战给米罗带来的痛苦。

This simple detail shows a woman looking out at the viewer, with an anguished face. The figures at the bottom seem more aggressive; perhaps they represent the brutality of war, whereas the woman symbolizes an innocent victim.

这个简单的细节描绘了一个以极度痛苦的表情注视着观众的女人。底下的图形看上去更有攻击性，它们可能代表了战争的残酷，而这个女人则象征着无辜的受害者。

Barcelona Suite IV, 1944. This is one of 50 lithographs that made Miró famous.

《巴塞罗那组图(四)》(1944)，这是让米罗成名的 50 幅石版画之一。

Drawing By Chance
随性作画

This technique of random, imaginative drawing was used by Miró in his *Constellations* series. He gave all these works descriptive, poetic names, such as *The Nightingale's Song at Midnight and the Morning Rain*, or *People in the Night Guided by the Phosphorescent Tracks of Snails*.

在《星座》组画里，米罗使用了随意而富有想象力的绘画技巧。他用描述性的、富有诗意的名字给这些作品命名，比如《午夜的夜莺之歌和清晨的细雨》或《夜晚沿着泛着微光的蜗牛爬行轨迹行走的人们》。

Using a black pen, close your eyes and make a bold but random squiggle on a plain piece of paper. Now look at your line and allow your imagination to see shapes and pictures within the squiggle. Fill in or add to the shapes, using different colors and adding features such as faces or hair, but be careful not to hide the original black line completely. When you have finished, look carefully at all the images your have created on your paper. Try to give the picture a title that accurately describes and links all the elements within it, like the long titles that Miró gave to his *Constellations* pictures.

闭上眼睛，用一支黑色的笔在一张白纸上大胆地、随意地画出一条曲线。然后盯着你画的曲线，充分运用想象力，看看这条曲线能组成哪些形状和图案。用不同的色彩来填充或增补这些形状，也可以添加一些特征，如脸或头发。但是小心，不要完全遮盖住原来的黑色线条。画完后，仔细看看你在纸上创作的所有形象，参照米罗给《星座》组画中的图画所起的长长的名字，试着给你的画也起一个名字——这个名字能够精确地描述画中所有的元素，并且把它们联系在一起。

GRAPHICS AND CERAMICS
制图与制陶

Only Picasso came close to Miró in the range of materials and references he used to make pictures, sculptures, ceramic designs, stage sets, and prints. Miró enjoyed working as a team with other craftspeople; for example, he combined printers' technical knowledge with his imagination to explore a huge range of surfaces and effects.

在创作绘画、雕塑，进行陶器设计、舞台设计，以及制作版画的材料和引用素材方面，能在多样性上和米罗媲美的就只有毕加索了。米罗乐于和工匠们一起工作。比如，他曾把印刷工人的技术和他的想象力结合起来，由此探索出了大量不同的外观和效果。

Aidez l'Espagne, 1937. With simple power, Miró's picture expresses the fears and determination of the Catalan people.

《帮助西班牙》（1937），此画具有简单的力量，表达了加泰罗尼亚人民的恐惧和决心。

BEGINNINGS IN PRINT
版画的开端

Miró's earliest prints had been made to illustrate a book of poems called *L'Arbre des Voyageurs* by the poet Tristan Tzara in 1929. In the following years he had created designs for many of the greatest poets in Europe. When, in 1937, Miró had made his powerful print *Aidez l'Espagne*, he had realized the power and popular appeal of print. He liked the fact that affordable prints could convey art throughout society, when such opportunities had previously been available only to the rich.

米罗最早的版画作品是 1929 年为诗人特里斯唐 · 查拉的诗歌集《旅行者的树》所创作的插图。

One of Miró's lithographs for Tristan Tzara's ***Parler Seul***, 1948-1950.

基于诗人特里斯唐 · 查拉的作品《自言自语》而创作的石版画之一（1948—1950）。

在之后的几年间，他为欧洲许多伟大的诗人进行过设计创作。1937 年，米罗创作了颇具震撼力的版画作品《帮助西班牙》，他也因此意识到版画作品中蕴含的力量和版画对人们的吸引力。以前只有富人才能拥有艺术品，而现在，价格低廉的版画能使艺术在全社会传播，这一点让他雀跃不已。

The Effects Of Fame
名声的效应

The *Barcelona Suite* spread the name of Miró around the world after 1942. His new interest in prints meant that he could design even more spontaneous compositions. He sent his ideas to a team of print makers to publish, and so could travel and create widely available art at the same time, increasing his status as a truly international artist.

1942 年以后，米罗因《巴塞罗那组图》而享誉全球。创作版画这一新的爱好为他设计出更自然的构图创造了条件。他把构思发送给一批印染商去印刷出版，这样他就能在四处游历的同时创作出深入大众的艺术，这也提升了他作为一名真正的国际化艺术家的地位。

When working with ceramics, an artist can use differing textures, such as this thick paint. This is one of 200 plaques that Miró made with Artigas in the late 1940s.

当用陶瓷作为创作材料时，艺术家可以使用不同的材质，比如这种厚重的颜料。这是米罗和阿蒂加斯在 20 世纪 40 年代末一起创作的 200 块饰板之一。

Estela de doble care, 1956.
《艾斯特拉的双重护理》（1956）

Ceramics And Pottery
陶瓷和陶器

The ceramicist Josep Llorens Artigas and Miró shared a friendship that went back as far as 1915. During the Second World War they met again. At Artigas's ceramic studio, Miró noticed a pile of imperfect pottery that lay broken by the kiln. He was immediately interested by the lack of control in the heat of a kiln, and by the infinite variety of chance effects in the firing process. In the 1950s Artigas built new kilns near Miró's studio, outside Barcelona. To Miró, ceramics were a mixture of sculpture and painting, allowing him to use color and work in three dimensions at the same time.

陶瓷艺术家约瑟夫·罗伦斯·阿蒂加斯和米罗的友谊可以追溯到1915年。在第二次世界大战期间，他们再次相遇。在阿蒂加斯的陶瓷工作室里，米罗看到了一堆被烧窑烧坏的有瑕疵的陶器。刹那间，他对烧窑热量的不可控制性以及因此产生的烧制过程中的随机效果产生了极大的兴趣。20世纪50年代，阿蒂加斯在米罗位于巴塞罗那郊区的工作室旁边造了新的烧窑。对米罗来说，陶瓷是雕塑和绘画的结合，让他可以同时运用色彩和手工来进行三维创作。

Respond To Sound
对声音的反应

Miró's many illustrations for poetry used this technique to echo the variety of feelings and moods within each poem, so creating a piece of art that was perfectly in tune with the meaning of the words.

米罗为诗歌创作的许多插图都使用了这种技巧来回应每首诗的不同感受和情绪，他也因此创造出了一种与诗歌文字相一致的艺术作品。

Find a piece of music that contains many different moods. For example, a good piece to choose is Ravel's *Bolero*. It is the same tune played continuously but by a series of individual instruments, to create a variety of sounds and atmospheres. While listening to the music, draw on a large piece of paper a line or colors that best represent the sound you are hearing. Think of the pitch and rhythm of the sounds, and the feelings that the music stirs in you. Use flowing or sharp lines and different colors. If the music is lively and snappy, you could draw zig-zag lines or dots. Red or orange might be good colors to choose. If it is sad and slow, try flowing, smooth lines and dark colors. Now try this technique with a poem. Ask a friend to read it out loud and "draw the poem" as he or she does so. As with the music, choose shapes and colors that correspond to the moods of the poem. Perhaps you could make a book of illustrated poems with your friends.

找一首包含不同情绪的乐曲。比如，你可以选择拉威尔的《波莱罗舞曲》。在这首乐曲中，一系列不同的乐器持续演奏出相同的旋律，从而创造出不同的声音效果和氛围。在聆听乐曲的时候，在一大张纸上画出能代表你所听到的声音的线条或颜色。画的时候要考虑一下音乐的音调和节奏，以及这首曲子给你的感受。用流畅、尖锐的线条和不同的颜色来作画。如果音乐很生动、很明快，你可以画上“之”字形的线条或圆点，红色或橙色是比较适合的颜色。如果音乐很悲伤或节奏缓慢，那么你就要试着用流畅、平整的线条和深色来创作。然后，试着把这种技巧用到诗歌上去。请一位朋友大声地朗读一首诗歌，同时，你要“把这首诗歌画出来”。与听音乐作画一样，选择与诗歌所表达的情绪相一致的形状和颜色。或许，你可以和你的朋友一起制作一本诗歌的插画作品集。

INTERNATIONAL FAME
国际声誉

For the first two years after the war, Miró remained relatively unknown while he continued to experiment with a variety of styles. In 1947 he traveled to New York. Although he was stimulated by his experience of the United States and was received there enthusiastically, his painting was not greatly influenced by the country.

在第二次世界大战结束后的两年里，由于米罗不停地尝试各种风格，故而变得相对低调。1947 年，他去纽约旅行。尽管美国之行对米罗有所启发，而且他受到了热情款待，但美国并未给他的画风带来显著的影响。

A WARM WELCOME
热烈欢迎

Miró's art was already known in New York, where there had been a retrospective of his work in 1941. When he arrived he was eagerly greeted by his old Surrealist friends who had settled there, such as Marcel Duchamp. The art world also appreciated Miró's work greatly, because he looked for new forms of expression that had no reference to traditional art forms. Almost immediately he was commissioned to paint a mural,

99 feet (30 m) squarc, in the dining room of the Terrace Plaza Hotel in Cincinnati.

米罗的艺术在纽约已经广为人知。早在 1941 年，这里就举办过他的作品回顾展。当米罗抵达纽约时，他那些已经在此定居的超现实主义老朋友们，比如马塞尔 · 杜尚，热情地接待了他。艺术界也非常欣赏米罗的作品，因为他探究的新的艺术表达形式和传统的艺术形式截然不同。他几乎一到美国就接到委托，为辛辛那提露台广场饭店的餐厅创作一幅长 99 英尺（30 米）的正方形壁画。

Woman and Bird in the Night, 1945, shows Miró's spontaneous style.

《夜晚的女人和鸟》(1945)， 体现了米罗的自然风格。

A Variety of Media
不同的介质

By this time, Miró's paintings comprised two categories. He described the first as his "slow paintings," in which he took care to make his lines perfect, as in his earlier works such as *The Farm*. The second type of painting was completely spontaneous. In both types he paid great attention to the painting's background. This could be made of almost anything: burlap, board, brown wrapping paper, or canvas, under which might be laid wire or plaster that stuck through the painted surface. One of Miró's favorite devices was to poke string through from the back and knot it at the front of the picture. There was almost no material or medium that Miró did not explore - he even used black currant jam to create a picture on one occasion.

到这个时期为止，米罗的绘画包含两个种类。他把第一种称为“慢绘画”，在这种类型的画作中，他对于线条的处理十分精细完美，例如他的早期作品《农庄》。第二种绘画类型则是完全自然随意的。在这两种类型中，他都在图的背景上花了不少心思。背景可以是任何材质，包括粗麻布、纸板、棕色的包装纸、帆布，在下面放置钢丝或石膏，把它们和画作表面粘贴在一起。米罗最喜欢的装裱方式是从后面戳线，然后在图的前方打个结。米罗所探索的材料和介质无所不包，他有一次甚至在创作一幅画时使用了黑醋栗酱。

Miró did not want to control this vast range of materials and styles, to make them a permanent feature of his work, or to perfect the use of them. He simply explored their potential as ways of creating new, exciting forms of art that could be groundbreaking and accessible at the same time.

米罗并不想把这么多材料和风格变成他作品的永久特点，也并不想要将这些材料和风格运用得尽善尽美。他只是想探索一下，看看能不能用这些材料和风格创造出一种新的、令人兴奋的艺术模式。这种艺术模式既是革新的，同时也是浅显易懂的。

The Smile of Flaming Wings, 1953, shows the refined lines and careful coloring of Miró's "slow paintings."

《燃烧的翅膀的微笑》（1953），展示了米罗"慢绘画"的精细线条和细腻的上色。

To create the painting's mottled effect, Miró has scrubbed down the canvas as far as the weave. Some areas are more intense. The light and dark patches around this star emphasize it within the picture.

为了创造绘画的斑驳效果，米罗在帆布上进行刮擦，直到织物暴露出来。有些地方的效果可能更为强烈。这颗星星周围浅色和深色的色块起到了突出星星的效果。

A Return To France
回到法国

In 1947 Miró returned to Paris, where he received a warm welcome after his long absence. The Galerie Maeght held a retrospective of his work, which increased his position as an international artist.

1947 年，米罗回到了巴黎。在离开多年之后，他的回归受到了热烈的欢迎。梅格画廊举办了米罗作品的回顾展，提升了他作为国际化艺术家的地位。

Miró then returned to Barcelona, where he entered into a period of enormous artistic output. He produced 55 paintings and more than 150 finished drawings between 1949 and 1950, as well as numerous uncompleted sketches and designs.

米罗后来又返回了巴塞罗那。在那里，他进入了一个艺术上高产的阶段。在 1949 年到 1950 年期间，他创作了 55 幅油画以及 150 多幅完整的素描作品，同时还创作了大量未完成的速写和设计。

Create Art On A Strange Surface
在特殊表面上创作

Miró experimented with a wide range of backgrounds to his paintings.

米罗在画作中尝试了很多不同的绘画背景。

Explore the effects of drawing or making a collage on an unusual background. Use anything you can find: a supermarket bag, a stone, an old record, a tile (shown here), or a piece of textured wallpaper, for example. Each background will affect the look and atmosphere of your picture, and may influence the subject you choose.

探索一下在不同寻常的背景上作画或者拼贴产生的效果。使用任何一种你能找到的材料：一个超市购物袋、一块石头、一张老唱片、一块瓦片（如图所示）或质地粗糙的墙纸等。每种背景都会对你的作品的外观和氛围产生影响，也可能会影响你所选择描绘的对象。

SCULPTURE
雕塑

Miró saw sculpture as a way of taking art to all people, saying: "I want to try... to go beyond easel painting... and get nearer to the masses of whom I have never ceased to be aware." Other people, such as his friend Joan Prats, saw sculpture as a wide field within which Miró could work. Prats observed: "When I pick up a stone, it's a stone. When Miró picks up a stone, it's a Miró."

在米罗看来，雕塑是把艺术带给所有人的一种方式。他说："我想尝试……画架以外的作品……更加贴近那些我无时无刻不在关注着的群众。"在诸如胡安·普拉提斯等朋友们的眼中，雕塑是米罗可以进行创作的一个广阔领域。普拉提斯评论说："当我捡起一块石头，那只是一块石头。但当米罗捡起一块石头，那就是米罗的一个作品。"

Personage with Three Legs, 1967. Miró liked the image of an agricultural fork, which was a very common tool in rural Catalonia.

《三条腿的人》（1967），米罗喜欢叉状农具的外形，这是加泰罗尼亚常见的一种农具。

PUBLIC MONUMENTS
公共雕塑

The use of "objets trouvés" (found objects) in Miró's art of the 1930s had more to do with the development of surrealism than with pure sculpture. In the 1950s Miró again returned to sculpture, but now based it on chance shapes and images. Miró's most famous sculptures date from the 1960s. In 1968 an enormous exhibition took place in Barcelona, where every aspect of Miró's work was displayed. The city also commissioned three monumental sculptures from Miró.

Sun Bird, 1968, was first cast in bronze, and later carved in marble.

《太阳鸟》（1968），初次创作的时候为铜铸，后用大理石雕刻。

20世纪30年代，米罗在作品中对“拾得物”的使用不仅关乎单纯的雕塑，还和超现实主义的发展有关。20世纪50年代，米罗重拾雕塑艺术，但这一次，他是在偶然的形状和图案基础上进行创作的。米罗最出名的雕塑作品可以追溯到20世纪60年代。1968年，巴塞罗那举行了一场盛大的艺术展，展出了米罗在艺术创作中各个方面的作品。巴塞罗那市还委托米罗创作了三个地标性雕塑。

These included a 197-foot (60-m) high sculpture on the hills overlooking the city, a pavement design to extend the length of the city's main road, the Ramblas, and a mural at the Barcelona airport. Miró was inspired by the simplicity of traditional Catalan sculpture. Yet his use of "objets trouvés" showed how he saw all materials and objects as useful.

这三个作品包括一个从山顶俯瞰整个城市的、高60米的雕塑，城市主要步行街兰布拉大街延长段的路面设计，以及巴塞罗那机场的一幅壁画。加泰传统雕塑的简洁给米罗带来了灵感，而他对于“拾得物”的使用则表明在他眼中，所有的材料和物件都是有用的。

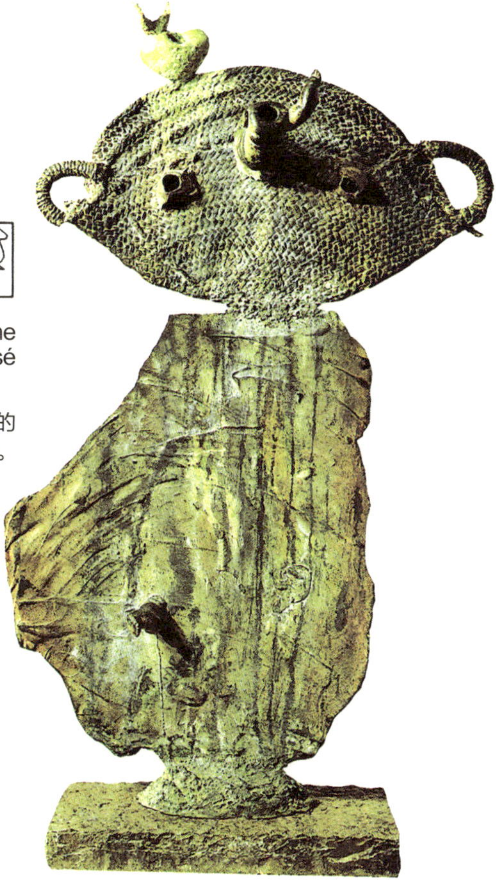

Personage and Bird, 1968. The rough patina was added by José Parellada.

《人物和鸟》（1968），其粗糙的铜绿表层为何塞·帕雷拉达所添加。

Everlasting Art
永存的艺术

Once his arrangements assembled, Miró would have them cast in bronze. The structures would thus become fixed and long lasting, and could be reproduced easily if necessary. Miró enjoyed the new textures that other materials brought, as well as the “chance” occurrences of casting. Once set, the bronze could be decorated with a patina (for example a film of copper) or changed by weather. In some cases, Miró painted the bronze.

在作品装配完成以后，米罗会用铜对它们进行铸造。这样，作品的结构可以得到固定并长久保持；如果需要，还可以便捷地复制。米罗很喜欢“偶发”的铸造创作，也很喜欢其他材料提供的新质地。铸造过程一旦结束，就可以在表面镀上薄层（比如一层薄薄的紫铜）来装饰铜器，或者让铸件表面随季节变化而风化。有时候，米罗还会在铜器表面作画。

Mixing Media
混合介质

Miró was interested in what happened when one art medium crossed into another. He enjoyed the different effects created by placing the same sculpture inside a room and outside.

将一种艺术材质融入另一种后会发生什么，米罗对此深感兴趣。他常常把同一个雕塑作品拿到室内和室外摆放，欣赏由此产生的不同效果。

CAPTURING SPACE
捕捉空间

Miró saw sculpture as affecting the space it used, and changing the space it sat within. The fork rising above the sculpture on page 60 prongs the sky above; without it this piece would be quite different and would not dominate the space so strongly. In 1964 Miró was given the chance to explore sculpture within space, when the Maeght Foundation was established on the hillside of Saint Paul de Vence in Provence. Among trees, surrounded by water, and set against the sea to one side and hills inland, Miró made sculptures of which the object itself was only a small part; it was the space and the natural landscape around the works that gave them their beauty and power. Each sculpture was placed carefully within the grounds of the Foundation so that it complemented the other works and the walls of the building as well as sat comfortably and dramatically within the beautiful natural surroundings.

米罗认为雕塑能影响它使用的空间，并能改变它所在的空间。第60页的雕塑上的叉子指向了上方的天空；如果没有这个叉子，这件作品将会很不相同，也不会那么强势地占据空间。1964年，米罗有机会探索空间里的雕塑。那时，梅格艺术基金会在普罗旺斯的圣保罗德旺斯的山腰上建立了。这个地方树木繁茂，四面环水，一边毗邻大海，内陆则是山地。在米罗创作的雕塑中，物体本身只是很小的一部分，作品周围的空间和风景才是赋予它们力与美的主要部分。每个雕塑都被小心地摆放在基金会的地面上，这样就能使每件作品都与其他作品和建筑物的外墙形成互补，舒适而引人注目地坐落在优美的自然环境中。

Sculpting In Space
空间里的雕塑

In his sculpture Miró was always very keen to experiment with the space occupied by each piece, and how its appearance and meaning were affected by placing it in different surroundings and next to a variety of objects.

在米罗的雕塑作品中，他总是致力于对每个作品所处的空间进行实验创新。他想知道当作品被放置在不同的环境中或者和许多不同的物体放置在一起时，其外观和含义是否会受到影响。

Find various objects with different textures and interesting shapes, and arrange them to make an unusual shape or figure. Remember that certain objects may remind you of something that could give your sculpture symbolic meaning; for example, Miró saw the shape of an agricultural fork as a symbol for the lives and feelings of the peasants of Catalonia. Like Miró, you could color with paint or dye to make the most important parts of the sculpture stand out. Set your work in various indoor settings, then place it outside against a building, the sky, or some trees, and see if your impression of your sculpture changes. Almost all sculpture is made to stand on the ground. Why not be different and hang it from some rafters or the branch of a tree?

找一些材质各异、外形有趣的不同物体，把它们放置在一起组成特别的形状或图案。记住，有些物体能让你产生一些联想，这些联想能使你的雕塑具有象征含义。比如，米罗把叉状农具看作代表加泰罗尼亚农民生活和感受的符号。像米罗一样，你也可以用颜料或染料来突出雕塑最重要的部分。把你的作品放到不同的室内背景里，然后把它放到室外，比如放到建筑物前、放到天空下，或放到树林里，看一看你对这个作品的印象会不会发生改变。几乎所有的雕塑都是立在地上的，那么你何不做些改变，试试把它悬挂在椽子上或树枝上呢？

Acclaim At Home
家乡的喝彩

In his 1975 works for La Défense in Paris, Miró used abstract forms to show emotions.

在 1975 年为巴黎的拉德芳斯中心商务区创作的作品中，米罗运用了抽象的形态来表达情绪。

In 1956 Miró saw the fulfillment of a dream he had held for over twenty years. His good friend, the architect José Luis Sert, designed a large studio for him outside Palma. In 1959 he received an award from President Eisenhower. After 1959 Miró's paintings became almost completely abstract. In the late 1960s the idea of a Miró Foundation was explored by Joan Prats, but Prats died in 1970. Sert later built the Foundation. Miró became more and more recognized by the world.

1956 年，米罗实现了他二十多年来的梦想。他的好朋友——建筑师何塞 · 路易斯 · 塞尔特——为他在帕尔马郊外设计了一间大型工作室。1959 年，他受到了时任美国总统艾森豪威尔的嘉奖。1959 年以后，米罗的油画几乎完全抽象化了。在 20 世纪 60 年代晚期，胡安 · 普拉提斯曾提议设立米罗基金会，但普拉提斯在 1970 年过世了。后来，塞尔特建立了这个基金会。米罗在世界上的知名度因此越来越高。

ENORMOUS CREATIVITY
极大的创造力

For much of the 1950s Miró had been engaged in sculptural and ceramic projects, but in 1959 he began to paint with renewed vigor, producing more than 100 canvases in a year. He expanded his visual language to mix together different techniques and symbols that he had previously used only separately. For example, the types of fine line that he had used in the *Constellations* series were set against pure color backgrounds, where previously they had been painted on mottled effects. The bold, almost violent lines of his gloomy prewar period were now mixed with delicate images of stars against bright colors. Miró used blemishes, imperfections, or manufacturers' trademarks on a canvas as a starting point for inspiration, or threw pots of paint onto the surface, in a way similar to Jackson Pollock. This allowed him to explore even further the artistic possibilities of chance effects.

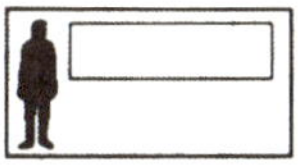

For Emili Fernández Miró, 1963. Miró used both bright colors and fine lines.

《致艾米丽·费尔南德斯·米罗》（1963），米罗同时使用了明亮色和精细线条两种手法。

在20世纪50年代的大部分时间里，米罗致力于进行雕塑和陶器作品创作，但是从1959年开始，他重新拾起了对油画的兴趣，在一年之内完成了一百多幅油画。他把之前独立运用的不同技巧和符号融合到同一个作品里，从而拓展了自己的视觉语言。比如，他将之前在《星座》组画中所运用的精细线条放到纯色背景上，而这种线条以前是画在色彩斑驳的背景上的。米罗在第二次世界大战前的一段时期里使用的那种近乎狂暴的粗线条，如今与精细的星星图案相结合，并且以明亮色为背景。米罗用画布上的污渍、瑕疵或生产商的商标作为灵感的开端，或把一罐颜料倒在画布上开始创作，这和杰克逊·波洛克的手法不谋而合。这种手法让他能够深入探究随机效果在艺术上的可能性。

Recognition In Spain
被西班牙认可

For Miró, 1968 was a special year. The vast retrospective exhibition and public monuments in Barcelona celebrated his achievements for the first time in his own country, as Franco's Fascist regime was coming to an end. Having been acclaimed worldwide, Miró had come home to stay.

对米罗来说，1968年是特殊的一年。声势浩大的作品回顾展和巴塞罗那的地标性雕塑设计都是祖国对他的成就的首次赞颂。而在这一年，佛朗哥的法西斯政权也走到了尽头。虽然那时米罗已经蜚声国际，但他还是选择回到家乡定居。

JOAN MIRÓ

胡安·米罗

In ***The Gold of the Azure***, 1967, Miró creates variety but maintains order.

《蔚蓝的光芒》(1967)，米罗在进行多样元素创作的同时也保持了一定的画面秩序。

This simple picture, from one of Miró's most productive periods, explores the enormous range of textures available within different colors. Thick bold lines, thin fine lines, blue, viscous red, and pure yellow are all combined within it.

这幅简单的绘画创作于米罗最为高产的时期，他在这幅画中探索了大量不同色彩的质地。画中汇集了厚重大胆的线条和细腻精巧的线条，以及蓝色、黏稠的深红色和纯净的黄色。

DEMOCRATIC ART
民主艺术

It would be a mistake to look deeply for lots of meaning or messages in the work of Miró. He wanted people to be able to interpret his work in their own way. Miró's paintings, tapestries, and sculptures were for everyone – nobody needed a particular intellectual background to enjoy his work, just eyes with which to see – making it a truly democratic art. This does not mean that Miró was not a skilled artist; it took him decades to make his images so clear, unique, and immediate.

试图在米罗的作品中深入探究其蕴含的意义或信息是徒劳的，因为他更希望人们能够用自己的方式解读他的作品。米罗的油画、挂毯画和雕塑是面向大众的——任何人只要专注于双眼所见，不需要运用特殊的学科背景知识就能欣赏——这使他的作品成为真正民主的艺术。但这并不意味着米罗是一个毫无技巧的艺术家；他花了几十年的时间，努力使笔下的形象更清晰、更独特、更直接。

EXPRESSIVE ART
有表现力的艺术

In many of his later works, like the sculptures for La Défense (see page 68), Miró represented the feelings and expressions of his subjects by using abstract, exaggerated features and gestures, such as large eyes and sweeping body movements.

在米罗的很多后期作品里，比如为拉德芳斯创作的雕塑（见第 68 页），他用抽象、夸张的特征和姿态来展现他对主题的感受和表达方式，例如大眼睛和扭曲的体态等。

Practice this form of exaggerated representation by looking at pictures of sports figures in the newspaper. Trace their faces or dramatic movements, then exaggerate your drawn line so that its shape expresses the person's emotions, such as the joy of a winning athlete. Then draw some imaginary people in this way, emphasizing features that reveal their personality. A greedy person might have a large mouth and hands, while a sad person could be shown with big, tearful eyes and a stooping body. Cartoonists use this sort of distortion all the time, to show extreme emotions like surprise, anger, happiness, and sorrow. Try to take this further to express more subtle ideas like energy, patience, or effort.

你可以通过观察报纸上的运动员照片来练习这种夸张的表达方式。留意他们的面部表情或剧烈运动时的体态，然后用夸张的线条来塑造形象，以表达这个人的情绪，比如获胜时的兴奋。用这种方式再画几个你想象中的人物，强调能显示他们个性的特征，比如贪婪的人会有大大的嘴巴和手，悲伤的人则会有一双眼泪汪汪的大眼睛和弯曲的身体。漫画家经常使用这种失真的手法来表达极端的情感，如惊讶、愤怒、幸福和悲伤。尝试进一步使用这种手法来表达更微妙的概念，如活力、耐心或努力。

THEATER AND TAPESTRY
戏剧和挂毯画

Throughout his life, Miró had worked in many fields of art - sculpture, ceramics, and printing as well as painting. By nature he was a modest man who liked teamwork. He therefore greatly enjoyed making set and costume designs for plays and ballets, which closely complemented the script or music. He also worked as part of a team when making his monumental tapestries, which were always carefully designed to match and enhance the surrounding architecture.

纵观米罗的一生，他在许多艺术领域都颇有建树，包括雕塑、陶器、版画以及油画等。从本质上说，他是一个谦逊的人，喜欢团队合作。因此，他很喜欢为话剧和芭蕾舞剧做布景设计和服装设计，而且他的创作能很好地适应剧本或音乐。另一方面，他也作为团队的一员，参与地标性挂毯画的创作。这些挂毯画通常设计精细，用来匹配并烘托周边的建筑物。

BEGINNINGS IN THEATER
戏剧的开端

Miró had first become involved with the theater as early as 1926, when he had designed and painted the set for the Russian Ballet's production of *Romeo and Juliet*, with the Surrealist painter Max Ernst. Unfortunately, no records of these designs have survived.

米罗初涉戏剧领域的时间可以追溯到 1926 年。

那一年，他和超现实主义画家马克斯·恩斯特一起为俄罗斯芭蕾舞剧《罗密欧与朱丽叶》设计并绘制了舞台布景，可惜这些设计没能留存下来。

THE BIRD OF LIGHT
光之鸟

A few years later, a dance choreographer, Léonide Massine, saw some of Miró's brightly colored abstract paintings. Massine realized that Miró would be able to express the imaginative world of children in a set for his ballet *Jeux d'Enfants* ("Children's Games"). Miró designed the set, toys, and costumes for the ballet, which was first performed in 1932. For Miró, the opportunity to work on such a large scale was very exciting; he saw the ballet as a huge picture with moving parts. In 1978 the Claca theater company asked Miró to design costumes for *Mori el Merma*, about a brutal dictator

Miró continued to create new works throughout the final years of his life.
晚年的米罗还在继续创作新的作品。

named Ubu Roi. The theme of bullying leaders reminded Miró of Franco, and he designed powerful, grotesque, and shocking costumes for the production. Miró's last work in the theater, in 1981, was almost autobiographical. He designed the costumes for a dance called *Miró, l'Uccello Luce* ("Miró, the Bird of Light"). The music, by Sylvano Bussotti, and the script, by Jacques Dupin, described the three main stages in Miró's career: his search for an artistic identity; his imaginative "dream world" period; and his final discovery of a versatile, unique artistic language.

几年后，编舞家莱奥尼德·马辛看到了一些米罗用明亮色彩绘制的抽象画。他意识到，米罗应该能够在他的芭蕾舞剧《孩子的游戏》中表达儿童富有想象力的世界。米罗为这出芭蕾舞剧设计了布景、玩具和服装，该剧于1932年首演。对米罗来说，有机会从事那么大规模的创作是非常激动人心的；他把芭蕾舞剧看作一幅由可移动的元素组成的大型画作。1978年，克拉卡戏剧公司邀请米罗为一出关于残酷的独裁者乌布罗伊的戏剧《Mori el Merma》设计服装。独裁统治者的主题让米罗想起了佛朗哥，于是他为这出戏设计了怪诞且具有视觉冲击力的服装，以此展示独裁者的强权。米罗最后一次参与戏剧作品创作是在1981年，这部作品几乎就是他本人的自传。他为这部名叫《米罗，光之鸟》的舞剧设计了服装。舞剧的作曲为希尔瓦诺·布索蒂，剧本由雅克·杜宾创作，描述了米罗艺术生涯中的三个主要阶段：探求自身艺术特质的阶段，富有想象力的“梦想世界”阶段，以及最终发现多元化的、独特的艺术表达方式的阶段。

WEAVING HIS ART
编织艺术

Miró's interest in tapestry came from the idea of three-dimensional pictures. In the early 1970s he would thread wool and other materials through loosely woven backgrounds like jute or sackcloth. Various "objets trouvés" could then be stitched or tied to the picture.

米罗对于挂毯画的兴趣源于他想要创作三维图画的想法。在20世纪70年代早期，他就尝试把羊毛和其他材料编织到像黄麻或粗麻等织得很疏松的背景板上。之后，他又尝试了把各种各样的"拾得物"缝制或系到图画中的做法。

Blemishes and marks on the cloth were included in Miró's tapestries, and he sometimes burnt the work, and then stamped out the flames to see what patterns were left. In the last decade of his life, Miró designed some huge, shaggy tapestries whose imaginative, bold colors and lines recall his later paintings.

在米罗的挂毯画中，污渍和印迹也是作品的一部分。有时，他会点燃作品，然后把火扑灭，看看会留下什么样的图案。在人生的最后十年中，米罗设计了一些巨型的、蓬乱的挂毯画，这些作品均富有想象力，运用大胆的色彩和线条，令人想起他后期的绘画作品。

Sobreteixim VI, 1972, is paint, rope, and wool on a jute mat.

《编制作品第六号》（1972），用油彩、绳子和羊毛创作于黄麻毯上。

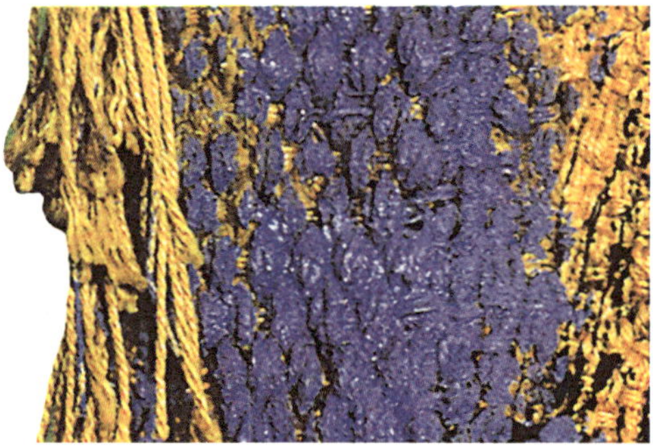

In common with his paintings of this period, Miró continued to use strong, pure colors and powerful lines. In this tapestry, a sense of depth has been created by stitching string and cord onto the canvas and adding paint and thread.

在这个阶段，米罗的绘画作品大多继续使用浓重的、纯净的色彩和有力的线条。在这幅挂毯画中，米罗把绳子和线圈缝制到帆布上，再涂上油彩，加上线头，从而使作品有了层次感。

MAKING TAPESTRY
制作挂毯画

Like Miró, you can use burlap, netting, or any other material with holes as background.

像米罗一样，你可以用粗麻布、网状织物或任何有洞的材料来做底板。

Thread colored string, cotton, or strips of old material through the background. You can copy the stitches shown here or make up your own effects. Try to build up blocks of color and differing textures, and stitch over the top of these with embroidery thread. Do not attempt to burn your picture.

把彩色的绳子、棉花或旧材料上的带子缝制到底板上去。你可以模仿这里的图来缝制图案，或者自行创造出属于你的效果。试着使用色块和不同的材质，用绣花线在底板上进行缝制。注意：不要尝试点燃你的画。

CHRONOLOGY OF MIRÓ'S LIFE

1893	April 20: Born in Barcelona, Spain.
1907	Attends the Escuela de Bellas Artes.
1911	Works as an accountant; falls ill.
1912-1915	Attends Francisco Galí's school.
1918	First solo show, at Galerías Dalmau in Barcelona.
1919	Visits Paris.
1921	Solo show in Paris.
1921-1925	Meets many artists and thinkers.
1925	Highly successful show in Paris.
1926	Galerie Surrealiste opens in Paris.
1926	Designs set for *Romeo and Juliet*.
1928	First visit to the Netherlands.
1929	Marries Pilar Juncosa.
1932	*Jeux d'Enfants* first performed.
1933-1936	Family settles in Barcelona.
1937	Spanish Civil War begins; Miró's family flees Spain.
1939	Outbreak of Second World War.
1940	Family settles in Majorca.
1941	Large-scale retrospective in New York.
1944	Starts ceramic work with Artigas.
1947	First visit to New York.
1947-1954	Achieves worldwide status.
1955-1958	Ceramics at UNESCO building, Paris.
1956	Settles in studio at Palma.
1960-1968	A period of high artistic productivity.
1964	Maeght Foundation opens, with sculptures by Miró.
1968	Exhibition in Barcelona.
1972	Creation of Joan Miró Foundation.
1978	*Mori el Merma* performed.
1981	*L'Uccello Luce* performed in Venice.
1983	December 25: Miró dies.

米罗生平年表

1893	4 月 20 日：出生于西班牙巴塞罗那
1907	在官方艺术学院学习
1911	从事会计工作；生病
1912-1915	在弗兰西斯科·伽利的学校学习
1918	在达尔默画廊举办首次个人展
1919	访问巴黎
1921	巴黎个人展
1921-1925	结识了很多艺术家和思想家
1925	巴黎展取得巨大成功
1926	超现实主义画廊在巴黎开业
1926	为《罗密欧与朱丽叶》设计舞台布景
1928	首次访问荷兰
1929	与皮拉尔·琼珂萨结婚
1932	《孩子的游戏》首演
1933-1936	米罗一家定居巴塞罗那
1937	西班牙内战爆发；米罗一家逃离西班牙
1939	第二次世界大战爆发
1940	米罗一家定居马略卡
1941	纽约大型回顾展
1944	和阿蒂加斯一起开始陶艺创作
1947	首次访问纽约
1947-1954	享誉世界
1955-1958	为位于巴黎的联合国教科文组织大楼进行陶艺创作
1956	在帕尔马的工作室定居
1960-1968	艺术高产期
1964	梅格艺术基金会成立，米罗为之进行了雕塑创作
1968	巴塞罗那展
1972	胡安·米罗基金会建立
1978	《Mori el Merma》公演
1981	《光之鸟》在威尼斯公演
1983	12 月 25 日：米罗逝世

A BRIEF HISTORY OF ART

The world's earliest works of art are figurines dating from 30,000 B.C. Cave art developed from 16,000 B.C. In the Classical Age (500–400 B.C.) sculpture flourished in Ancient Greece.

The Renaissance period began in Italy in the 1300s and reached its height in the sixteenth century. Famous Italian artists include Giotto (ca. 1266–1337), Leonardo da Vinci (1452–1519), Michelangelo Buonarroti (1475–1564), and Titian (ca. 1487–1576).

In Europe during the fifteenth and sixteenth centuries, Hieronymus Bosch (active 1480–1516), Albrecht Dürer (1471–1528), and El Greco (1541–1614) produced great art. Artists of the Baroque period include Peter Paul Rubens (1577–1640) and Rembrandt van Rijn (1606–1669).

During the Romantic movement, English artists J. M. W. Turner (1775–1851) and John Constable (1776–1837) produced wonderful landscapes. Francisco Goya (1746–1828) was a great Spanish portrait artist.

Impressionism began in France in the 1870s. Artists include Claude Monet (1840–1926), Camille Pissarro (1830–1903), and Edgar Degas (1834–1917). Post-Impressionists include Paul Cézanne (1839–1906), Paul Gauguin (1848–1903), and Vincent van Gogh (1853–1890).

The twentieth century has seen many movements in art. Georges Braque (1882–1963) painted in the Cubist tradition. Salvador Dali (1904–1989) painted in the Surrealist tradition. Pablo Picasso (1881–1973) was a prolific Spanish painter at the forefront of modern art. More recently, Jackson Pollock (1912–1956) and David Hockney (1937–   ) have achieved fame.

艺术简史

世界上最早的艺术作品是小雕像，可追溯到公元前 30000 年。公元前 16000 年，洞穴艺术开始发展。在古典时期（公元前 500—公元前 400），雕塑在古希腊得到了繁荣发展。

在意大利，文艺复兴时期开始于 14 世纪，到 16 世纪发展至鼎盛时期。著名的意大利艺术家包括乔托（约 1266—1337）、列奥纳多·达·芬奇（1452—1519）、米开朗琪罗·博纳罗蒂（1475—1564）和提香（约 1487—1576）。

在欧洲，在 15 世纪到 16 世纪期间，耶罗尼米斯·博斯（活跃期为 1480—1516）、阿尔布雷希特·丢勒（1471—1528）以及埃尔·格列柯（1541—1614）都创作了伟大的艺术作品。巴洛克时期的代表艺术家有彼得·保罗·鲁本斯（1577—1640）和伦勃朗·凡·莱因（1606—1669）。

在浪漫主义运动中，英国艺术家约瑟夫·马洛德·威廉·透纳（1775—1851）和约翰·康斯太勃尔（1776—1837）创作了绝佳的风景画。弗朗西斯科·戈雅（1746—1828）则是一名伟大的西班牙人物肖像画家。

19 世纪 70 年代，印象主义在法国萌芽，代表艺术家有克劳德·莫奈（1840—1926）、卡米耶·毕沙罗（1830—1903）和埃德加·德加（1834—1917）。后印象主义画家包括保罗·塞尚（1839—1906）、保罗·高更（1848—1903）和文森特·梵高（1853—1890）。

20 世纪，艺术领域出现了许多运动。乔治·布拉克（1882—1963）是传统立体主义画风的画家。萨尔瓦多·达利（1904—1989）是超现实主义画家。巴勃罗·毕加索（1881—1973）是一名高产的西班牙画家。另外，杰克逊·波洛克（1912—1956）和大卫·霍克尼（1937—）也是 20 世纪知名的画家。

MUSEUMS AND GALLERIES

The following museums and galleries have examples of Miró's work:

England:

Tate Gallery, *London*

France:

Alexander Calder Collection, *Sache*

Musée du Louvre, *Paris*

Galerie Maeght, *Paris*

Musée Nationale d'Art Moderne, *Paris*

Germany:

Folkwang Museum Collection, *Essen*

Wallraf-Richartz Museum, *Cologne*

Italy:

Peggy Guggenheim Foundation, *Venice*

Spain:

Joan Miró Foundation, *Barcelona*

Maria Delors Miró Collection, *Palma*

Sweden:

National Museum, *Stockholm*

United States:

Albright-Knox Art Gallery, *Buffalo, New York*

City Art Museum, *St. Louis, Missouri*

Cleveland Museum of Art, *Cleveland*

The Solomon R. Guggenheim Collection, *New York*

Museum of Modern Art, *New York*

Philadelphia Museum of Art, *Pennsylvania*

博物馆和美术馆

以下博物馆和美术馆中存有米罗的作品：

泰特美术馆，英国伦敦

亚历山大·考尔德收藏馆，法国萨舍

卢浮宫，法国巴黎

梅格画廊，法国巴黎

法国国立现代艺术博物馆，法国巴黎

弗柯望博物馆，德国埃森

瓦尔拉夫－里夏茨博物馆，德国科隆

佩吉·古根海姆收藏馆，意大利威尼斯

胡安·米罗基金会，西班牙巴塞罗那

玛丽亚·德洛尔·米罗收藏馆，西班牙帕尔马

国家博物馆，瑞典斯德哥尔摩

奥尔布赖特－诺克斯美术馆，美国纽约水牛城

城市艺术博物馆，美国密苏里州圣路易斯

克里夫兰艺术博物馆，美国克里夫兰

所罗门·R. 古根海姆博物馆，美国纽约

现代艺术博物馆，美国纽约

费城艺术博物馆，美国宾夕法尼亚州

GLOSSARY

Abstract art

Paintings that consist entirely of patterns and shapes, and do not attempt to portray anything in the real world.

Avant-garde

A phrase used to describe something that is ahead of its time.

Collage

Building up a picture from pieces of colored material or paper.

Cubism

An art movement, dating from 1907, in which paintings and sculptures were broken up into distorted shapes. The artists used muted colors and showed subjects from more than one angle.

Dada

An art movement that included poetry, theater, and music as well as painting, and rejected traditional ways of creating art.

Fascism

A political movement headed by a dictator that places the nation above the individual and forcibly suppresses opposition.

Fauvists

This name was given to a loose-knit group of artists who painted in vivid colors in around 1905-1908.

Lithographs

Prints made from a stone print surface rather than a linoleum or metal one.

Nationalism

Focusing on the interests of one's own country or area above all others.

Republicanism

Favoring a form of government without a monarch.

Retrospective

An exhibition, usually on a large scale, that looks back at the work of one particular artist over many years.

Surrealism

An art movement (including poetry and theater) based on the exploration of dream worlds and the subconscious.

术语表

抽象艺术

指完全由图案和形状组成的绘画，其目的不在于描绘真实世界中存在的事物。

先锋

用来形容超前于其所处时代的事物。

拼贴画

用一些彩色材料或纸片拼凑在一起的图画。

立体主义

指一项艺术运动，始于 1907 年。立体主义的绘画和雕塑都被拆解开来，碎裂成失真的形状。艺术家用哑色从不同的角度展现主题。

达达主义

指一项艺术运动，包含诗歌、戏剧、音乐和绘画，排斥传统的艺术创作形式。

法西斯主义

指由独裁者领导的政治运动，无视个体权益，强势镇压反对势力。

野兽派

指 1905 年到 1908 年期间，一群用鲜活的色彩进行创作的艺术家们，但这个群体比较松散。

石版画

在石头表面而非油毡或金属表面上创作的版画。

民族主义

指过分重视本国或本地区的利益，无视其他国家或地区的利益。

共和主义

指支持无君主的政府组成形式。

回顾展

指一种展览，通常规模很大，用来回顾某个特定的艺术家在过去许多年里的作品。

超现实主义

指一项基于对梦境和潜意识的探究的艺术运动（包括诗歌和戏剧）。

INDEX OF PROPER NAMES

专有名词索引

INDEX OF PICTURES

图片索引

扫一扫，听赏析音频

SELECTED PAINTING（I）
精选画作赏析（一）

《丑角的狂欢》

创作于 1924 年到 1925 年，现收藏于美国纽约水牛城诺克斯美术馆。

这是米罗在超现实主义时期最引人注意的和最富于他追求的超现实主义精神的代表作，是当时广受赞誉的第一幅超现实主义名画，这幅画的命名也十分恰当。

在这幅画里，米罗完全以自己的梦幻为主题，画作内容以他的故乡塔拉戈纳省的风景为主。这幅画完全是作画者对梦境中幻象的表现，当时有记者访问他，他解释说当一个人饥饿到某一种程度时就会产生幻觉。

这幅作品非常可爱，有一种颠倒空间的奇异想法，说来也是非常特殊的。这张画描绘的是狂欢节时在一个室内的空间里进行的一场极端兴奋的群体集会，充满了生动的气氛。你看那块桌布就像要滑下来参与这生动的庆祝，那个梯子也像在跳跃似的，而这个“游戏”的中心人物小丑是这幅画的中心。此外，还有两个体形像猫一般的人物、一把吉他，以及一只站在骰子上的小虫子。各种稀奇古怪的幻觉一览无遗。你注意到了吗？窗户上似乎还有一只小昆虫也想进来参与活动。

米罗完成这张作品后，马上将之展出并轰动一时，很快就得到了大家的认可，被称为出色的超现实主义大师。

在米罗的这幅画中，小丑有一张圆脸，由红和蓝两种不同的颜色构成。在画作上方离我们较远的地方有一只眼睛，代表了一个人。在这只眼睛周围，米罗用故乡的红土色作为背景，运用蓝色的地方都是细心思考过的。其实米罗并没有给这幅画任何特别的意义，他只想把我们梦幻中异乎寻常的想象和颇具创新意味的自然界画出来。所有这些小东西都很不合形式逻辑地被安排在画中的各个位置上。米罗喜欢用符号来代表他的日常生活，他认为这比真实的情景更有效。

超现实主义主要分为抽象派和形体派（用一种变形虫的形象来代表自然界原生态和想象的结合）。米罗是走向后一派的画家。

扫一扫，听赏析音频

SELECTED PAINTING（Ⅱ）
精选画作赏析（二）

《农庄》

创作于 1922 年，现收藏于美国华盛顿国家艺术馆。

米罗是西班牙超现实主义艺术家，他的创作形式十分多元。他十分热爱位于西班牙塔拉戈纳省蒙特罗奇小镇上的父母的农场。在他的一生中，他创作了各种不同的艺术作品，诸如油画、雕塑、编织物、舞台布景、公共场所的塑像，来表达他内心的情感。这使他成为一个出色的国际性的艺术家。

《农庄》这幅画是让米罗一举成名的作品之一。这是他在 29 岁时描绘的位于故乡的农场，是他生活经验的浓缩，也是他梦想中家园的写照。这幅画展出时，他已稍有名气，但此时画却无人问津，直到 1925 年，美国文学家海明威（也是米罗的好友）用 5000 美金购下此画。米罗的画风十分特别，他几乎将他记忆里故乡所有可能存在的特征都放入此画。这是一幅田园风格的作品，许多肉眼看不见的结构，诸如埋在地下的小镇排水道系统，他也画了进去。同样的道理，米罗会把太阳画在天空，以代表当地的气候，可是他的作品里却没有任何阴影。他的这种想法及新的作画风格，在当时跟其他的印象派画家完全不同。当时，印象派艺术家只注重他们四周环境的一面，米罗却将他所知道的全部真实情景均画入作品里。从他的作品中，我们找不出也看不到任何其他人的影响或是技巧。因此，这幅作品展出时成为大家注意的焦点。然而，尽管大家都注意到他的绘画风格与印象派不同，但此画还是乏人问津、无人收藏。米罗所用的结构主题不完全是理想化地让此画的结构显得合理，相反，他想把所有存在的结构表达无遗。这就是他成为超现实主义画家的起步。

作家海明威非常欣赏米罗，也十分喜爱此画。在他去世后，其夫人将此画捐赠给华盛顿国家艺术馆，作为他们的永久馆藏品。

■ 画作赏析由但孟新撰稿，阿达演播。

Special thanks to Joan Miró Foundation, Barcelona; Joan Miró Foundation, Palma de Majorca; Bridgeman Art Library; Frank Spooner Pictures; Design and Artists Copyright Society; ADAGP, Paris; The Estate of Joan Miró.

特别感谢

胡安·米罗基金会，巴塞罗那；胡安·米罗基金会，马略卡岛帕尔马；布里奇曼艺术馆；弗兰克·斯布纳画院；设计和艺术家版权协会；法国图像及造型艺术著作人协会，巴黎；胡安·米罗私宅。